My Soul

by

Dawn Brown

ISBN: 1-4140-6677-5 (e-book)
ISBN: 1-4140-6678-3 (Paperback)

Printed in the United States of America
Bloomington, IN

This book is printed on acid free paper.

1st Books - rev. 01/14/04

MY DEDICATION

THIS BOOK IS DEDICATED TO, FIRST, AND FOREMOST, GOD! HE IS MY HEAVENLY FATHER! WITHOUT HIM I WOULD NOT BE HERE. HE IS THE ONE WHO CREATED ME, GAVE ME THE WORDS TYPED ON THESE PAGES. SECOND, MY WONDERFUL HUSBAND, WHO GAVE ME HIS LOVE, SUPPORT, AND FRIENDSHIP UNSELFISHLY! THIRD, MY CHILDREN AND GRANDCHILDREN WHO HELPED ME THROUGH IT ALL WITH THEIR HUMOR AND WISDOM. ALSO, THE LIFE THAT GOD GAVE ME FROM BIRTH UNTIL NOW, IS RE-CREATED ON THESE PAGES. I THANK EVERYONE FOR THEIR SUPPORT, LOVE, AND KINDNESS. MY FRIENDS WHO ENCOURAGED ME, AND MY FAMILY WHO STOOD BY ME. BUT MOST OF ALL, I THANK GOD FOR JESUS, WHO HAS REDEEMED ME FROM MY SINS. WITH ALL THE GRATITUDE AND LOVE, I THANK EVERYONE FROM THE BOTTOM OF MY HEART!

Table of Contents

INTRODUCTION

TO ENTER INTO THE GATES OF YOUR SOUL, ONE MUST FIND THE KEY TO ONE'S OWN HEART. ACCEPTING EXCEPTIONS OF THE TERMS OF LIFE. NOT BELIEVING THE STANDARDIZATION OF NORMALCY. FOLLOWING DEPTHS OF CIRCUMSTANCES. ALWAYS ASKING AND LOOKING FOR THE UNKNOWN. ONCE THE GATES ARE OPENED, NO STONE WILL BE LEFT UNTURNED. NO BURIAL WILL BE AFFIRMED, UNTILL THE HEART IS FULLY PREPARED.

ONE MUST KNOW THE TRUE SELF. ONE CAN ONLY HOPE OF WHAT TO LET OUT AND WHAT TO KEEP HIDDEN. THE KEY LIES WITHIN THE HEART. WHEN THE HEART CAN NO LONGER SURVIVE, THE SOUL IS HERE FOR ETERNITY. WHEN SURVIVAL IS LOST, THE KEY TO THE SOUL MUST BE UNLOCKED.

TROUBLESOME HEARTS ARE FROM LIFELONG EXPERIENCES, NOT EVER KNOWING IF ALL THE PIECES WILL FIT TOGETHER. WE WILL NEVER KNOW BEFOREHAND WHAT CARDS LIFE HOLDS FOR US. ALL WE CAN DO IS ACCEPT AND LEARN. THE OLDER ONES ARE THE WISER ONES. WE HAVE TO BE CAREFUL AND NOT LOSE OURSELVES IN THE LIFE PROCESS. ONE HAS TO ACCEPT SELF, BEING AWARE OF ONE'S OWN SOUL. KNOWING WHAT TO HOLD IN, LOCK AWAY, AND WHAT TO BE LET KNOWN. THE ONLY ONE THAT CONTAINS THIS POWER IS SELF. SELF ALONE HAS THE KEY, THE POWER, TO ACCOMPLISH LIFE'S CIRCUMSTANCES. THIS WILL DETERMINE WHAT KIND OF PERSON, AND WHAT WOULD YOU WANT TO ACCOMPLISH IN LIFE. ACCEPTANCE OF SELF IS THE MOST IMPORTANT PROCESS OF ALL. YOU ALONE

HAVE THE POWER TO CONTROL, HATE OR PRIDE? DEPENDING ON LIFE, ONLY YOU CAN ANSWER WHAT WILL BE ACCOMPLISHED AND WHAT WILL BE DESTROYED.

TO CREATE ONE'S OWN MASTERPIECE, THE SKILL OF POWER MUST BE USED. THE COMPLIANCES OF POWER MUST WISELY BE USED. IF THE ARRAY OF CONFUSION IS ALLOWED, THE POWER WILL BE LOST. WISDOM IS NOT GIVEN. WISDOM COMES FROM EXPERIENCE. EXPECTATIONS OF WISDOM IS VERY DEMANDING. WHEN OVEREAGERNESS MAKES ITSELF KNOWN, PATIENCE IS THE KEY TO WISDOM. PATIENCE IS A MUST. TO DENY SELF OF THIS WOULD BE CRUCIAL TO THE HEART OF REALITY. REALITY NOT SEEN WITH A TRUTHFUL EYE, IS VERY DESTRUCTIVE. TO MAKE ONE'S OWN ACCOMPLISHMENTS, ONE MUST LISTEN.

THE POWERS WITHIN MUST WISELY USED, OR THE DESTRUCTION OF POWER WILL TAKE OVER. THE POWER WAS GIVEN TO US BY THE EXTREME DIVINE. BE AWARE OF THOSE POWERS AND HOW THEY ARE USED. THERE IS NO ESCAPE, NO MATTER HOW FAR THE EXTREMITY TAKES YOU.

THE SKILL OF POWER IS BENEFICIAL TO THE SOUL. THE POSITIVE ASPECTS OF OUR SKILL WILL BE NONSTOP. OUR UNIQUENESS AND INDIVIDUALITY IS THE MAKING OF WHO WE ARE, AND NOT NECESSARILY WHO WE WANT TO BE.

TAKING TIME TO DEVELOP OUR OWN PERSONAL SKILL AND POWER, IS VERY DEMANDING, AT TIMES OVERWHWELMING. THE KEY IS PATIENCE, SLOWING LONG ENOUGH TO DEVELOP THEM. THE INSIDE OF THE SOUL CANNOT BE DECEIVED, NOR CAN IT BE TORN. THE SOUL IS THE ONLY ONE THAT KNOWS THE TRUTH OF REALITY.

THE SOUL REIGNS FOREVER.

THE ONE TRUE GIFT THAT IS GIVEN, IS LIFE. WE ARE TAUGHT THE BASICS. THE COMPLEXITY COMES FROM WITHIN, WHICH CANNOT BE DENIED. THE SOUL IS AN ENDANGERED SPECIES, BECAUSE TRUTH TO SELF IS CONSISTENT.

EXPERIENCES OF THE HEART CAN DESTROY HUMANNESS, BUT STRONGLY SUPPORT THE SOUL. IT IS DURING THESE TIMES THAT ONE MUST NOT LOSE SIGHT OF WHERE STRENGTH COMES FROM. ONE MUST HUMBLE THEMSELVES AND BE THANKFUL FOR OUR ONE TRUE GOD

TO WHAT INDICATION LIFE HOLDS NO BOUNDARIES, NO ONE KNOWS. LIFE IS PREDESTINED FROM DAY OF CONCEPTION. TAKING LIFE FOR GRANTED IS DANGEROUS. LIFE IS GIVEN, BUT CAN BE TAKEN AWAY. THERE IS ONLY ONE CHANCE GIVEN, CAREFULLNESS ALONG WITH WISDOM MUST BE INSTATED. IF OUR WAY IS LOST, WE ARE EASILY REMINDED.

LIFE IS A LEARNING EXPERIENCE, WE LEARN, WE DISCOVER, THEREFORE WE GROW, UNLESS AN UNFORSEEN CIRCUMSTANCE KIDNAPS IT. OUR LIFE MAY BE SHORTENED OR LENGTHENED ACCORDING TO OUR INDIVIDUALITY. FROM WITHIN, COMES OUR STRENGTH AND WISDOM. OUR SKILLS AND KNOWLEDGE ARE LEARNED. THE WISE MAN KNOWS FROM WHENCE IT CAME, THEREFORE DOES NOT JEOPARDIZE IT.

LIFE IS A JOURNEY, AN ADVENTURE, BUT ALSO A TEST TO SEE HOW IT IS USED. IF WISELY USED, THE REWARDS ARE GREAT. IF POORLY USED, WARNINGS ARE NOT HEEDED, DESTRUCTION BEGINS. IT ISN'T WORTH TAKING LIFE INTO OUR OWN JUDGEMENT, FOR IT SHALL BE

GIVEN BACK TENFOLD. TO TREASURE LIFE IS A GIFT, TO GIVE LIFE IS A BLESSING, TO TAKE A LIFE, IS UNFORGIVABLE. IF LIFE IS TAKEN, BUT NOT BY ANY WRONGDOING, THEN THAT IS DESTINY. TO ACCEPT THE CHALLENGE OF DESTRUCTIVE CIRCUMSTANCES, IT IS UP TO US HOW WELL WE DO BOTH MENTALLY, AND PHYSICALLY.

TROUBLESOME TIMES OF THE HEART, CAN DAMAGE POWERS. IT CAN SLOW THE PROCESS OF WISDOM. IT CAN STRENGTHEN SKILLS OF SELF. TO KNOW ONE'S TRUE SELF IS AN ACCOMPLISHMENT. OVERCONFIDENCE LEADS TO BREAKDOWN OF OPERATIONS. TO HAVE SELF CONFIDENCE IS A BLESSING. WE ARE NOT TO LET THE POSSESSION OF DARKNESS ENTER OUR DOMAIN. IT NOT ONLY BELONGS TO US, WE BELONG TO OUR CREATOR. DO NOT LET INTERVENTION OVERWHELM, OR CONTROL. THIS DECEPTION CAUSES THE BREAKDOWN. NOT KNOWING WHERE OR HOW, CAN DEVESTATE ABILITIES, AND SKILLS. THIS CAUSES EXCRUCIATING TORTURE.

THE TORTURE CAUSED BY POSSESSION, TAKES ITS TOLL ON ALL RESOURCES OF HUMANITY. THIS DOES NOT EXCLUDE THE HEART. THE HEART IS THE LINK TO ALL RESOURCES, INCLUDING WISDOM. IF THE HEART IS TAKEN BY POSSESSION, THE SOUL WILL HAVE TO INTERVENE.

THE HEART OF RIGHTEOUSNESS, IS THE WISDOM OF LOVE. SOUL DEPTHENING LOVE, HEALS ALL WOUNDS. IT CAREFULLY CHOOSES ITS PLACE, GUARDED BY THE SOUL. IT CAN ALSO BE DECEIVED.

DECEPTION HAS MANY FORMS, ITS MOST COMMON FORM IS FRIENDSHIP. TO THE NAKED EYE CANNOT BE SEEN, NOR CAN IT BE HEARD. AS IT SLITHERS SLOWLY THROUGHT THE MIND, IT IS OF

CONTROLLING THE MIND, HEART AND SOUL OF HUMANS. HOWEVER THE SOULCANNOT BE CONTROLLED. IT WILL CLOSE THE DOOR TO DECEPTION. ALL FUNCTIONS OF THE HEART AND MIND WILL CEASE. IT WILL ABSORB ALL CONTENTS OF THE MIND. IT SILENTLY CREEPS THROUGH THE HEART, GAINING ALL OF ITS MATERIAL. AFTER ALL IS TAKEN, EMPTINESS AND DESPAIR WILL REMAIN.

WHEN DECEPTION HAS TAKEN ALL, THE KEY OF SOUL MAKES ITSELF ADVERTLY KNOWN. IF AND WHEN THE KEY IS USED, THEN, AND ONLY THEN, WILL SOUL TAKE CONTROL. THE SOUL IS FOREVER, NEVER DISAPPEARING, ONLY LOCKING ITSELF AWAY INTO THE DEEP CORNERS OF THE BODY. WHEN THE SOUL IS UNLOCKED, THE SUNLIT STREAMS OF THE HEART, WILL COMMUNICATE WITH THE MIND TO REJUNEVATE ITSELF. THE BLANKET OF NATURE WILL SHIELD ITSELF AGAINST DECEPTION. IT WILL BRING WARMTH AND CAREGIVING TO THE RIGHTEOUS HEART, SPREADING WISDOM THROUGH ITS ENTIRE SHIELD.

EXPECTATIONS OF WISDOM CAN BECOME OVERANXIOUS, BEING CAREFUL NOT TO OVERWHELM. CONTROL OF THE HEART AND MIND WILL ALWAYS BE TRUE TO ETERNITY. TRUE SELF WILL NEVER DIE, THE SOUL WILL REIGN FOREVER. THE SOUL WILL LET SELF MAKE DECISIONS ON ITS OWN ACCORD, ABSORBING KNOWLEDGE FOR SAFEKEEPING. IT MAY BE NEEDED FOR PURPOSES UNKNOWN TO MAN. IT IS KNOWN TO THE SPIRITUAL SELF. FOR YOURSELF TO KNOW, EXPLORE THE SOUL OF REALITY. REALITY IS THE KEY TO LIFE, FANTASY IS THE KEY TO LOVE.

WITHOUT GETTING THESE CONFUSED, TO LIVE IN A FANTASY, WILL CAUSE GREAT DANGER TO THE REALITY OF LIFE. NOTHING

KNOWS THIS BETTER THAN DECEPTION. THIS IS HOW IT TAKES CONTROL.

CONTROL IS ITS ONLY PURPOSE, SPARING NOTHING IN ITS PATH. DESTROYING ALL THAT IS FAMILIAR AND CONCEIVED. THE SOUL KNOWS THIS ALL TOO WELL. WHATEVER IS CONCEIVED BY THE SOUL, DECEPTION WILL DESTROY, IF GIVEN AN OPEN WINDOW. NO WINDOW CAN BE LEFT OPEN TO DECEPTION, OR IT WILL BECOME SWINE. THE DEVESTATING EFFECT TO THE HEART AND MIND, WILL HAVE ADVERSE REACTIONS.

NO STONE WILL BE LEFT UNTURNED, BUT THE REJUVENATION OF THE HEART AND MIND CAN BECOME COMPLETE WITH THE HELP OF SOUL. WHEN THE LIGHT ENTERS INTO THE WINDOW OF DECEPTION, IT WILL BE COMPLETELY DESTROYED, UNTILL THE CIRCUMSTANCES OF LIFE OVERTURN THE REJUVENATION OF POWERS.

THE PURPOSE OF BEING, LIES WITHIN ONE QUESTION. WHO, ON GOD'S WONDERFUL CREATION, CAN ANSWER THE QUESTION OF LOVE? WHO CAN ANSWER THIS QUESTION WITH DEPTH AND UNDERSTANDING? MANY HAVE TRIED, BUT THE PURPOSE STILL REMAINS A MYSTERY. NO ONE CAN REALLY EXPLAIN THEIR PURPOSE OR HOW THEY CAME TO BE. EVERYONE HAS ASKED THIS QUESTION AT LEAST ONCE IN THEIR LIFE. IT CAN ONLY BE EXPLAINED THROUGH THE GREATEST BOOK EVER WRITTEN, "THE BIBLE".

CLOSE EXAMINATION OF ONE'S OWN LIFE, CAN TEAR INTO THE MIND, AS WELL AS DESTROY! MAKING THE HEART AS COLD AS A STONE. THIS CAN LEAD TO CLOSING ALL DOORS AND LEAVING THE WORLD BEHIND. IT IS A CONFORMANCE OF ECCENTRICITY. IT IS LIKE A WOMAN, FOR THE PLACIDNESS OF HER FAMILY, WILL SACRIFICE

HERSELF, BECOMING VIRTUALLY NONEXISTENT.

THE PURPOSE AND EXISTENCE, DOES NOT DEPEND ON ANOTHER, BUT DOES DEPEND ON SELF. SELF-EXAMINATION IS THE TRUE ROLE TO EXISTENCE. ALTHOUGH EXISTENCE IS BEARABLE, SURVIVAL IS COMMON, BUT THE PERSON AS A WHOLE CANNOT BE TOLERATED. THE EVIL THAT LURKS WITHIN, CAN POSSESS ONE'S EXISTENCE AT ANY MOMENT. WHEN THIS HAPPENS, DESTRUCTION IS CLOSING IN.

THE CRIES OF THE SOUL AR SILENCED BY THE POSSESSION OF DARKNESS. THE WINDOWS CAN NO LONGER BE OPENED. TERRIFYING SCREAMS OF THE HEART, ARE THREATENED BY THE THROBBING CLAWS OF INSANITY, REACHING INTO THE DEEPEST LIMITS OF THE MIND. SEARCHING TO SEEK AND DESTROY ALL COMFORT OF LIFE, BEING EVER SO CAREFUL, TO REACH EVERY LIMIT IT CAN. NO ONE CAN BYPASS THE EVIL WITHIN. THE ONLY WAY OF SIRVIVAL IS TO KEEP POSSESSION HIDDEN. KEEPING IT LOCKED AWAY, NOT LETTING ESCAPE BECOME COMPLETE. THE COMPLETION OF ESCAPE BECOMES EXCRUCIATING! NEVER RELEASING, OR COMPENSATING, FOR DESTRUCTION. WHEN DESTRUCTION BECOMES HONORED, THE SOUL WILL BURY DEEP WITHIN THE HEART. TRYING TO FIND SOLACE FROM A DESPERATE ISOLATION! TEARS, CAN NO LONGER FORM, SCREAMS ARE SILENCED, ONLY EMPTINESS, DESPAIR, AND DESTRUCTION, REMAIN TO TURN AN EMPTY, LIVING, BODY INTO A CORPSE!

THE COMPLICATIONS OF THE TORTURE OF LIFE, ARE TOO ENORMOUS. THE WATERFALLS OF THE MIND, ARE CONSTANTLY DRIPPING, NEVER SEEMING TO OVERFLOW. CONSCIOUSNESS DESIRES CONTEMOLATE TO THE HUMAN SPIRIT. ONCE IT IS GIVEN IN

TO, CONSEQUENCES TAKE OVER, AND ALL IS FORSAKEN. FUTURISTIC GOALS, DREAMS OF THE HEART, ARE ALL BURIED UNDER THE SEA OF LIFE.

A WOUNDED SOUL, A BROKEN SPIRIT, A LOST HEART, CAN LEAD TO DESTRUCTION. THE DEVESTATION OF LIFE, CAN LEAD TO THE ULTIMATE ACTION OF LEAVING IT ALL BEHIND. IF LIFE HOLDS SUCH MISERY, THEN WHAT IS THE PURPOSE OF IT ALL?

INSANITY OF THE MIND, IS WITHOUT CONTROL. ALL THOUGHTS ARE DELETED, AS IF, NONE WERE AVAILABLE. POSSESSION CREEPS IN SO SILENTLY THAT IT IS NOT KNOWN UNTILL DESTRUCTION, DEVESTATION, TEARS DOWN THE BEING OF HUMANITY. HUMANITY CANNOT SURVIVE, POSSESSION, UNLESS CONTROL IS TAKEN BACK BY THE SOUL! IF THE HEART IS TO SURVIVE, THEN CONSCIOUSNESS MUST RETURN!

TO KEEP THIS IN PERFECT ORDE, ONE MUST BE IN CONTROL, BEFORE ALL IS DESOLATE, AND DESPERATION IS THE ONLY FRIEND LEFT. THERE IS A SAYING THAT DESPERATE TIMES CALL FOR DESPERATE MEASURES. PAGE 3 BY: DAWN BROWN

TO KEEP SELF IN HARMONY WITH WHAT IS, ONE MUST NOT CONFUSE FANTASY WITH REALITY.

WHO IS TO SAY THAT FANTASY CANNOT BECOME REALITY? ONE MUST BE CAREFUL NOT TO GET LOST IN THIS ASPECT. CONFUSION IS A PART OF POSSESSION. JUST EXISTING, SURVIVING, IS ALSO A PART OF POSSESSION. LETTING POSSESSION IN AND BEING TRAPPED IS LOSING CONTROL. DO NOT BECOME DESTRUCTIVE, OR OVERWHELMED, DEATH WILL COME BEFORE IT SHOULD. TAKE A CLOSE EXAMINATION OF WHAT IS BEFORE YOU, BECAUSE THE TIME

IS AT HAND! THE REALIZATION OF FOCUS WILL FALL INTO PLACE.

IF ONE COULD UNDERSTAND AND COMPREHEND, THE TRUE MEANING OF LOVE, ONE WOULD FOCUS INTO REALITY. LOVE IS UNCONDITIONAL, ACCEPTING, CHERISHING, NOURISHING, GIVING SACRIFICING, COMPRISING, GROWING, CHALLENGING, DISCIPLINE AND SELF CONTROL. IT IS NOT OBSESSIVE, ABUSIVE, EMOTIONALLY DISTRUBING, JEALOUS RAGES, CONFLICTING, OR CONTROLLING IT IS BEING WHO YOU ARE, AND LETTING THE OTHER PERSON DO THE SAME. SELF CAN ONLY SURVIVE TO A CERTAIN POINT. THEN POSSESSION TAKES OVER. IT TAKES EVERY PART OF BEING, LEAVING TORMENT AND DESTRUCTION BEHIND. SHATTERING THE MIND, DESTROYING THE SPIRIT, AND BLEEDING THE HEART. THIS WILL LEAVE HUMANITY VIRTUALLY NONEXISTENT, NOR SURVIVING, JUST HOLLOW, CRITICISM OF SELF, HOPELESSNESS, AND WITHOUT DREAMS.

IT IS A SAD TRAGEDY WHEN THIS HAPPENS. BUT YET, THE BODY IS STILL BREATHING, NOT CARING WHAT HAPPENS. NOT CARING OF WHAT BECOMES. BECAUSE OF POSSESSION, AND DESTRUCTION, ONE BECOMES INVISIBLE.

THE PERILIOUS INVASION OF ONE'S TRUE SELF, IS VERY DEVESTATING. TO BE ABLE TO REACH ONE'S TRUE SELF, ONE MUST BE ACCEPTING OF ITS ENTIRITY. TO REACH THE ULTIMATE FANTASY.

THE PASSION OF DESIRE, LEADS TO THE BURNING OF THE SOUL, ACHING DEEP WITHIN. TRYING TO FULLFILL THE INNERMOST FANTASIES OF THE SPIRIT. BEING HUMBLE TO PURSUE THE FULLFILLMENT. TO COME INTO THE CONCLUSION OF PERFECTION. TO REACH THE ULTIMATE FANTASY, REACH DEEP WITHIN THE SPIRIT OF

SATISFACTION, AND RELAY THE UTMOST COMMUNICATION. BEING HONEST WITH SELFISHNESS, CONTROL, AND DETERMINATION. THE BEAUTY COMES FROM CREATIVITY, AND ACCEPTANCE. LIFE WILL BECOME MORE REWARDING THAN EVER, ONCE THE LIGHT ENTERS INTO THE WINDOW OF THE SOUL. THAT IS THE PURPOSE OF BEING!

MY SOUL

AS I TAKE A LOOK BACK ON MY LIFE, THE MEMORIES COME CLEARLY INTO FOCUS. THE PAIN, THE HORROR, THE ABUSE IS SO SCARRING, THAT WORDS CANNOT DESCRIBE IT. IT IS THROUGH ALL THE EMOTIONAL DISTURBANCE IN MY LIFE, THAT I HAVE BECOME WHAT I AM TODAY.

THROUGH ALL OF THIS, SOMETHING HAS DIED. I HAVE LOST A PART OF ME I FEAR WILL NEVER RETURN. THE HEART GETS BLED, THE MIND GETS SHATTERED, BUT THE SOUL WILL REMAIN.

IT IS THROUGH THE WINDOWS OF MY SOUL, THAT I AM LOOKING, ON THE OUTSIDE LOOKING IN. LOOKING AT MYSELF, ALWAYS SEARCHING, BUT NONEXISTENT. I FEEL I HAVE BECOME LIKE A ZOMBIE, DOOMED TO ROAM THE GRAVEYARD FOREVERMORE.

THE HOPE THAT HAS BEEN LOST, THE DREAMS THAT WILL NEVER BE BROUGHT BACK TO LIFE, AND THE TEARING OF THE MIND. THIS CAN DRAIN ONE OF ALL ASPECTS OF HUMANNESS. LEAVING ONE UNABLE TO FIGHT, TO SURVIVE AND HOLD ON TO WHAT IS INSIDE. WHAT ONE HAS TO REMEMBER, IS THAT POWER COMES FROM WITHIN YOURSELF. ONE HAS TO REACH DEEP DOWN INTO ONE'S SOUL, AND FIND THE KEY TO UNLOCK THE DOOR. THE SOUL IS THE KEY TO SURVIVAL. IT IS THE JOY OF LIFE. THE HAPPINESS OF LOVE. THE SORROW, WHEN UNEXPECTED CIRCUMSTANCES COME OUR WAY.

THERE IS NO ONE THAT HAS NOT EXPERIENCED THESE, BUT THE SOUL KEEPS US SURVIVING. ONE HAS TO REMEMBER HOW TO

UNLOCK THE DOOR, AND BRING TRUE SELF TO LIFE. DO NOT GET BURIED UNDERNEATH, BECAUSE IF ONE IS LOST IN THE SEA OF LIFE, ONE MIGHT NOT BE ABLE TO RETURN, ALWAYS REMEMBER, HOW TO UNLOCK THE DOOR TO YOUR SOUL!!!!!

MEMORIES

REMEMBERING ALL OF THE THINGS THAT I WAS TAUGHT. REMEMBERING THE VALUES, THE GIFTS THAT WERE GIVEN ME. THE MOST PRECIOUS GIFT OF ALL WAS LOVE, GIVEN TO ME BY MY GRANDMOTHER, AND GRANDFATHER. THEY GAVE ME VALUES OF HONESTY, SINCERITY, CHARITY, DISCIPLINE, AND HARD WORK.

NO ONE THAT I HAVE MET, CAN EXPLAIN, OR COMPREHEND THE TRUE MEANING OF LOVE. THE TRUE MEANING OF THE WORD LOVE IS GIVING. LOVE IS KINDNESS, HONESTY, SINCERITY, COMMUNICATION, TRUST, RESPECT, ADMIRATION, CHERISHING, NOURISHING, APPRECIATION, SUPPORT, ACCEPTANCE, AND MOST OF ALL, UNCONDITIONAL. FOR LOVE TO GROW, ALL ASPECTS HAVE TO BE MET. IF NOT, THEN LOVE WILL SURELY DIE.

PHYSICAL ATTRACTION IS NOT LOVE, IT IS LUST. PEOPLE HAVE A TENDENCY TO GET THEM CONFUSED. TRUE LOVE IS OF ACCEPTING THE BEAUTY THAT IS ON THE INSIDE.

THE PERSON WITHIN. IF THIS HAPPENS, THEN THE OUTSIDE WILL NOT MATTER.

IT IS A LOT OF WORK LOVING SOMEONE, BUT TRUE IS WORTH ALL THE GOLD IN THE WORLD AND THEN SOME. WHEN YOU FIND SOMEONE, AND REALLY FALL IN LOVE, NOT LUST, THEN LOVE WILL MAKE THE JOURNEY OF LIFE MORE PROSPEROUS THAN EVER BEFORE. THE REWARDS OF LOVING SOMEONE, AND HAVING SOMEONE TO LOVE, ARE FAR GREATER THAN THE IMAGINATION CAN TAKE YOU!!!!!!!!!!!

THE HEART OF TIMES

TIMES OF THE HEART CAN CHANGE A PERSON FOR A LIFETIME. TRAGEDIES, UNFORSEEN CIRCUMSTANCES, AND OBSTACLES OF FRIENDSHIPS, CAN TEAR AT YOUR HEART, UNTILL BIT BY BIT, IT GROWS AS COLD AS A STONE. A STONED HEART, CAN NO LONGER FEEL, FEED THE SPIRIT, OR UNLOCK THE DOOR TO THE SOUL. TO STAY AHEAD OF SELF, ONE MUST BE CAREFUL WITH THE HEART. GUARDING WITH OUNCE OF POWER THAT IS WITHIN SELF. THE COMPASSION, THE SENSITIVITY, AND EMOTIONS, MUST BE CAREFULLY GUARDED, OR IT WILL BE DOOMED TO ROAM THE BURIAL OF THE SEA OF LIFE FOREVER.

TO REGAIN HEALING OF THE SOUL, SPIRIT, AND HEART, THE POWER OF THE MIND MUST BE USED. MIND WILL CONTROL THE BODY. BUT ONE MUST ALSO USE THIS POWER TO HEAL ITSELF. TO GAIN CONTROL, ONE MUST KNOW THE TRUE SELF. OPENING DOORS TO THE SOUL, LETTING THE LIGHT ENTER INSIDE, SEARCHING THOROUGHLY, FOR ANY OBTRUSIONS. NO ONE CAN ESCAPE LIFE, NOR CAN ANYONE ESCAPE DEATH. BUT IT IS HOW WE DEAL WITH LIFE, AND WHAT LIFE WILL BRING TO US. WE MUST SEARCH OUR SOUL, TO KNOW OUR TRUE SELF. THIS IS WHERE OUR BEAUTY AND CONFIDENCE COMES FROM. THEY COME FROM WITHIN, TO SHINE, ON THE OUTSIDE. THE SOUL WILL SURVIVE ANYTHING. IT IS WHAT WE CHOOSE TO DO WITH OUR SOUL. IF OUR SOUL IS TORN, DAMAGED, OR LOST, WE CAN USE THE POWER TO HEAL OURSELF. TO GROW, THERE ARE EXPERIENCES WE MUST FACE, TESTS THAT MUST BE

TAKEN. EACH ONE WITH GREAT EXPECTATION, AND ANTICIPATION TO FACE THESE EXPERIENCES, AND TAKE THE TEST OF LIFE, WE MUST BE HEALED, AND KNOW OUR TRUE SELF.

THE MOST PRECIOUS GIFTS THAT ONE HAS, IS, HEART, SOUL AND MIND.THESE ARE GIFTS THAT MUST BE CHERISHED. DO NOT LOSE THEM, IF THEY ARE LOST, THEN IT WILL BE A SLOW PROCESS IN HEALING. TIME AND POWER CAN HEAL YOU, BUT IT IS A LONG PROCESS. IT IS VERY SLOW, NOT ONLY SLOW, BUT VERY LONELY. THE LONELINESS CAN BE VERY DEVESTATING TO YOUR SOUL. THAT IS WHY YOU HAVE TO BE CAREFUL, WHAT YOU LOCK BEHIND THE DOOR, AND WHAT IS KNOWN. ALWAYS LET THE BEAUTY, COMPASSION, SHINE. DO NOT BE TOO CONFIDENT, OR LONELINESS WILL TAKE OVER. LONELINESS IS TOO HARD TO FACE, ESPECIALLY WHEN THERE IS ONLY DARKNESS LEFT INSIDE. YOU HAVE TO LET THE LIGHT ENTER, TO START THE HEALING PROCESS. ONCE IT BEGINS, THEN THE WARMTH OF THE SPIRIT WILL FILL YOU, THE COMPASSION OF YOUR HEART WILL RETURN, AND THE DOOR OF YOUR SOUL WILL OPEN!!!!!

SURVIVAL

IT HAS BEEN MY EXPERIENCE OF SURVIVAL, MANY HEARTBREAKS, SORROW, PAIN, AND ABUSE. LIFE HAS A WAY OF BRINGING UNEXPECTED CIRCUMSTANCES TO ANYONE. WHAT ONE HAS TO REMEMBER, IS NOT TO LOSE THE MOST PRECIOUS GIFTS OF ALL. THE HEART, SOUL, AND MIND. THROUGH THESE EXPERIENCES OF MY LIFE, I HAVE EXPERIENCED LOVE, AND HAPPINESS. LIFE IS NOT A BED OF ROSES, BUT IT ISN'T A BED OF THORNS EITHER. THE KEY TO SURVIVAL IS THIS: THE POWER AND CONTROL OF THE MIND, THE SOUL, AND THE HEART.

TO CONTROL THESE, WE MUST FACE WHAT LIFE HAS TO OFFER. IT IS OUR CHOICE ON HOW WE ACCEPT THE CHALLENGES OF LIFE. PROBLEMS THAT COME OUR WAY, ARE JUST SOLUTIONS WITH WORK CLOTHES ON. NO CAN ACCEPT THESE FOR US, IT IS ALONE THAT WE MUST FACE THESE CHALLENGES.

IT IS THE ACCEPTANCE OF OURSELF THAT GIVES US THE POWER. WE MUST KNOW OUR TRUE ENTIRITY TO FACE THEM. COMMON KNOWLEDGE IS GIVEN, BUT WISDOM IS EARNED. RESPECT FOR HUMANNESS COMES FROM WITHIN. WE ARE ALL HUMAN, BUT WITH ALL DUE RESPECT, WE ARE ALL ALONE, TO FACE LIFE AND WHAT IT BRINGS OUR WAY. IT IS OUR CHOICE ALONE, IT IS OUR POWER WITHIN SELF THAT DETERMINES THE OUTCOME. ALWAYS BE PREPARED TO EXPECT THE UNEXPECTED, BY KEEPING THE DOOR TO YOUR SOUL UNLOCKED!!!

JOURNEY

WHAT I HAVE LEARNED THROUGH MY JOURNEY, IS THAT MISTAKES ARE MADE. THE PROBLEM WITH THE HUMAN RACE, IS THAT NO ONE WANTS TO FACE THE CONSEQUENCES OF MAKING A MISTAKE. THESE ARE MADE, AND CONSEQUENCES ARE GIVEN TO ENSURE OUR LEARNING. WE CAN LEARN, OR WE CAN RUN. WE CAN FORGIVE, FORGET, MOVE ON, OR DWELL ON THEM. SOMETIMES IT IS NOT EASY TO FORGET THE PAST, ESPECIALLY ONE AS HORRIBLE AS MINE. DO NOT LET IT GET IN THE WAY OF YOUR JOURNEY.

LIFE IS TOO SHORT TO BE MISERABLE, AND UNACCOUNTED FOR. WISHING I HAD DONE THIS OR THAT. JUST DO THE THINGS OF ENJOYMENT, LIVING LIFE TO THE FULLEST.

THERE IS A LOT OF PAIN, AND SORROW IN THIS WORLD. THERE IS ALSO A LOT OF JOY, SERENITY, AND PEACE, THAT THIS WORLD HAS TO OFFER. TO ACCOMPLISH OUR GOALS IN LIFE, WE HAVE TO BE DETERMINED, AND SET ON WHAT IT IS WE ARE TRYING TO ACHIEVE. SETTING OUR PATHS IN THAT DIRECTION, AND DOING IT. THERE MAY BE SETBACKS, OBSTACLES TO OVERCOME, BUT YOU ALONE HAVE THE POWER WITHIN TO DO IT. NO ONE ELSE CAN DO IT FOR YOU, IT HAS TO BE DONE BY YOU, AND YOU ALONE.

TO ACCOMPLISH THESE, THERE IS ONLY ONE WAY. ALWAYS REMEMBERING CONTROL, PRECIOUS GIFTS, AND KEEPING THE DOOR OF YOUR SOUL UNLOCKED!!!!!!

PAIN

STORY

TO TELL A STORY,

WITH DEPTH AND SPIRIT,

IS AN UNDERSTATEMENT,

THE HEARTBREAK,THE PAIN, THE SORROW,

THAT I HAVE SEEN, AND EXPERIENCED,

WORDS CANNOT DESCRIBE THE FEELINGS,

BURIED DEEP, WITHIN MY SOUL,

NOR CAN THEY DESCRIBE,

THE SUFFERING OF THE SPIRIT!

FEELING LIKE A ZOMBIE,

DOOMED, TO ROAM THE GRAVEYARD, FOREVERMORE!

WITH SHACKLES CHAINED AROUND MY HANDS AND FEET,

WITH THE RAIN, NEVERENDING,

THE CLOUDS OVERSHADOW ME,

IT IS DIFFICULT

TO PUT PIECES OF A JIGSAW PUZZLE

TOGETHER,

ONCE THEY ARE SCATTERED,

PIECES SEEM TO BE MISSING,

BUT ONE DAY,

MAYBE I CAN FIT IT TOGETHER.

AND WHEN IT IS,

WHAT A PICTURE IT WILL BE!!!!!!!!!!!!!

Dawn Brown

THIS THAT I AM

THE WEEPING WILLOWS OF MY SOUL,

ARE CONSTANTLY SEARCHING FOR THEIR EXISTENCE,

THIS THAT I AM,

I DO NOT WISH TO BE,

THIS THAT I WANT,

I CANNOT BE.

IT IS A STRUGGLE,

TO FIND PEACE,

DEEP, WITHIN MY SOUL,

ALWAYS SEARCHING,

BUT NEVER ACCEPTING,

THIS THAT I AM.

MYSELF,

I CANNOT BE,

LOSING, MY HEART, MY SOUL, MY MIND,

ALL WILL FALL INTO PLACE,

WITH THIS THAT I AM,

BUT I WILL NEVER RETURN.

THE UNBEARABLE PAIN,

WILL NEVER LEAVE ME,

LEAVING BEHIND,

THE BROKEN PIECES,

THAT WILL NEVER BE PUT TOGETHER,

My Soul

THIS THAT I AM,

I DO NOT WISH TO BE,

AND THIS THAT I WANT,

I CANNOT BE!!!!!!!!

Dawn Brown

LOATHSOME

LOATHSOME IS MY HEART,

HOLLOW IS MY BODY,

DARKNESS IS MY MIND,

LIKE A PRISONER,

IN SOLITARY CONFINEMENT.

NO LIGHT CAN ENTER,

NOR CAN IT ESCAPE,

TRAPPED,

LIKE A VETERAN AT WAR,

NO PEACE IS ACCEPTABLE.

EVERY BREATH I TAKE,

LEAVES ME IN EXCRUCIATING PAIN,

BUT I AM NOWHERE TO BE FOUND,

IN THE SILENCE OF DARKNESS,

A BROKEN SPIRIT,

A TRAPPED MIND,

THERE ISN'T ANY TIME LEFT

THE WAR IS A STRUGGLE,

AS IT POSSESSES ME,

NO PEACE ACCEPTABLE,

AS IT OVERWHELMS ME,

A FIGHT TO THE FINISH,

AS DESTRUCTION DEFEATS ME,

ALONE WITH NO HOPE,

My Soul

NO DREAM, NO LIGHT,

I CAN NO LONGER FIGHT,

ALL THERE IS LEFT,

IS SLEEP,

AS I CLOSE MY EYES,

THE WAR IS OVER!!!!!!

Dawn Brown

MY REALITY

THE DEEP, DARK, SHADOWS OF THE PAST,

CREEP IN UNEXPECTEDLY,

SURROUNDING,

SHATTERING,

MY MIND,

AS I WATCH IN HORROR,

EVERY SCENE,

THE CRACK OF THE BAT,

AGAINST MY BACK,

SENDS SHIVERS DOWN MY SPINE,

BLOOD RUNS SLOWLY,

DOWN MY FACE,

AS THE CRUMPLED GLASS,

CUTS AND TEARS AT MY SKIN,

SCREAMS ARE SILENCED,

BY THE RUGGED HANDS,

AROUND MY NECK,

THE THIN, LONG, BLACK WHIP,

STINGS MY LEGS,

LIKE A MILLION BEES ATTACKING ME,

I TAKE MYSELF TO A DESSERTED ISLAND,

FILLED WITH SOLITUDE AND PEACE,

WITH RAINBOWS UNDERNEATH,

WILL I EVER RETURN?

My Soul
YES, BUT FOR NOW,

I AM IN MY FANTASY,

TO ESCAPE THE TORTURE,

OF MY REALITY!!!!!!!!!!!!

LONELINESS

LONELY,

IS THE SOUL,

AS STORMINESS,

SILENTLY CREEPS IN,

DESTRUCTION OF THE MIND,

SHADOWS THE HEART,

OF A SHALLOW BODY,

TEARING INTO THE WEAKENED FLESH,

WITH ITS GNASHING TEETH,

COMPLETELY IGNORING,

THE VICTIMS CRIES,

WHEN WILL THIS HORROR END?

THERE IS NO TURNING BACK,

NO DEFEAT,

THE POWER IS TOO STRONG,

THE FORCE TOO OVERWHELMING,

GENTLY TAKING EACH BREATH,

INTO ITS SHARP CLAWS,

NEVER LETTING GO,

UNTILL SURRENDER IS ACCOMPLISHED,

NO MORE STRUGGLE,

NO MORE PAIN,

ONLY DARKNESS TAKES OVER,

WHERE HUMANITY USED TO BE,

My Soul

THERE IS NOTHING LEFT,

ONLY EMPTINESS,

DESPAIR,

AND DESTRUCTION!!!!!

Dawn Brown

THE GHOST

THE TEARDROPS,

ARE STREAMING DOWN MY FACE,

LIKE HONEYDEW,

ON SOFT, GREEN GRASS,

THE PAIN,

OF MY HEART,

LEAVES,

NO ROOM,

FOR A SOFT, EMBRACE,

THE GHOST,

THAT KEEPS HAUNTING MY MIND,

I CANNOT FIND,

HE GENTLY ENTERS,

WITHOUT KNOCKING,

NOT CARING,

IF ANYONE IS AT HOME,

SILENT WHISPERS OF MY MIND,

HE CAN ROAM,

BEING EVER SO CAREFUL,

TO LEAVE,

NO STONE UNTURNED,

IN MY MIND,

HE BURROWS AS DEEP AS HE CAN,

TO REACH INTO MY SOUL,

My Soul

TAKING TIME,

TO STRIP EACH PIECE,

TO WATCH IT BURN,

SOON,

THE LIGHT WILL ENTER,

TAKING ITS PLACE,

TO STOW AWAY,

THE GHOST,

THAT KEEPS HAUNTING MY MIND!!!!!

HUMANITY

THE WINDOWS OF MY SOUL,

ARE PIERCED,

BY THE THROBBING CLAWS,

OF INSANITY,

WRAPPING ITSELF AROUND ME,

LIKE A COBRA,

SQUEEZING,

UNTILL THERE IS NO MORE LIFE,

STRIKING,

AT EVERY BREATH I SOAK IN,

TEARING ME,

WITH ITS GNASING TEETH,

TORMENTING,

TORTURING,

UNTILL NOTHING IS LEFT,

TAKING CONTROL,

OF MIND, BODY, AND HEART,

CONSUMING MEMORIES,

LOVE,

HOPE,

HONESTY,

AND ALL OF LIFE,

THE SPIRIT CAN NO LONGER SURVIVE,

NOR CAN IT SURRENDER,

My Soul

CAUGHT IN THE WEB OF POSSESSION,

THE NET OF DESTRUCTION,

THERE IS NO MORE BEING,

OF,

HUMANITY!!!!

Dawn Brown

NOTHING

WHAT IS LEFT,

WHEN,

THERE ARE NO DREAMS?

NO HOPE?

WHAT HAPPENS,

WHEN

YOU LOSE HEART,

SOUL,

AND MIND?

SKELETON,

HOLLOW,

DESPAIR,

EMPTINESS,

DESTRUCTION,

AND DARKNESS.

THOUGHTS OF LEAVING THIS WORLD,

TO END THE PAIN,

THE HURT,

THE DESPERATION,

BUT THERE IS ONLY ONE LIFE,

ONE JOURNEY,

SO WHAT IS LEFT?

NOTHING!!!!!!!!!!!

THE PATH

NO ONE KNOWS WHY,

NOR CAN ONE EXPLAIN,

SADDENED CIRCUMSTANCES,

OR TRAGEDIES,

THAT IS JUST THE WAY THE PATH IS,

ONE DAY,

YOU GO ONE WAY,

ANOTHER DAY,

IS A DIFFERENT PATH,

IT MIGHT BE A LEFT TURN,

IT MIGHT BE A RIGHT TURN WITH A DANGEROUS CURVE,

BUT WHEN THERE IS A FORK IN THE ROAD,

YOU JUST KIND OF STAND AND STARE,

NOT KNOWING WHICH WAY TO TURN,

FEELING EMPTY,

LONELY,

AND NUMB,

NO HEART, NO SOUL, NO MIND,

JUST NUMB,

LIKE A ZOMBIE,

SEARCHING FOREVERMORE,

BUT NEVER FINDING,

ALWAYS HOPING,

BUT NEVER EXISTING!!!!

LOVE

HEART AND SOUL

HEART, SOUL, MIND, AND SPIRIT,

WHAT GOOD ARE THESE,

IF THEY ARE LOST?

WHAT IS A PERSON,

IF THEY HAVE NONE?

WHAT ARE FEELINGS,

WITHOUT A HEART?

WHAT IS A SPIRIT,

WITHOUT A SOUL? WHAT ARE THOUGHTS, WITHOUT A MIND? SET

THE SPIRIT FREE,

FROM ENTRAPPMENT,

SET THE MIND FREE,

FROM IMMORTAL THOUGHTS,

SET THE SOUL FREE,

FROM CAPTIVITY,

SET THE HEART FREE,

FROM PAIN,

ALL OF THESE,

WILL LEAD TO A LIFE,

OF LOVE, JOY, AND FAITH!!!!!

Dawn Brown

LOVE

THE GENTLE MOONLIGHT,

SOFTLY WHISPERS,

UPON YOUR TENDER FACE,

AS YOU LOOK AT ME,

WITH YOUR WARM SMILE,

YOUR EYES GLEAM,

WITH EXCITEMENT,

LIKE A CHILD AT CHRISTMAS,

AS I PRESS MY TENDER FACE,

SOFTLY AGAINST YOURS,

YOUR BODY IS SO WARM,

YOUR KISS IS SO SWEET,

LIKE HONEY FROM A FRESH BEEHIVE,

A WARM EMBRACE,

A GENTLE TOUCH,

LINGERS FOR SO LONG,

MY SPIRIT SOARS,

AS I SLOWLY CARESS YOU,

TEASING YOU,

MY HEART BELONGS TO YOU,

MY SPIRIT IS LIFTED,

MY BODY IS YOURS,

WITH TENDER, LOVING, CARE,

HOLDING YOU CLOSE,

My Soul

WITH MYSELF WRAPPED YOU,

WE ARE ONE,

NOW THAT YOU ARE INSIDE!!!!!

Dawn Brown

RAINBOW

THE PASSION,

THAT SURROUNDS ME,

ACHES,

DEEP WITHIN MY SOUL,

CRUSHING MY HEART,

LIKE A BLEEDING STONE,

BLINDING ME,

FROM THE SWEET VIEW OF LOVE,

WATCHING PEOPLE PASSING BY,

INSIDE,

BURNING LIKE AN OPEN FLAME,

TURNING ME INSIDE OUT,

NEVER LETTING GO,

NEVER ESCAPING,

UNTILL I FALL,

INTO THE WARM,

SOFT,

TENDER,

TOUCH,

OF THE RAINBOW!!!!!

FAITH

THE WINDOWS OF MY SOUL,

ARE ON FIRE,

WITH THE STEAMING RAYS OF THE SUN,

CUTTING DEEP,

LIKE A SHARP KNIFE,

THE DARKNESS,

LIFTED,

THE SILENCE,

BROKEN,

THE STORMS,

ARE PASSING,

WITH EACH MOMENT,

FLASHING BEFORE ME,

LIKE A HOLLYWOOD MOVIE,

HEALING ME,

WITH EACH BREATH I TAKE,

THE WOUNDS ARE SO DEEP,

THE CUT IS BAD,

WITH EVERY BEAT OF MY HEART,

I CAN FINALLY FACE,

THE REALITY OF WHAT IS,

THE SPIRIT,

OF THE BLINDING SUN,

PROTECTS ME,

LIKE A SOFT, WARM, BLANKET,

TAKING EVERY PART OF ME,

SOAKING ME,

SO THAT I CAN START ANEW,

FACING EACH DAY,

WITH LOVE,

HOPE,

HONESTY,

BUT MOST OF ALL,

FAITH!!!!!

MOTHER NATURE

Dawn Brown

SHORE

THE STEAMING RAYS OF THE SUN,

PIERCES MY SOUL,

LIKE A CALF BEING BRANDED,

THE COARSE SAND,

CRUMBLES UNDER MY FEET,

AS I WALK ALONE,

ON THE LOATHSOME SHORE,

I TAKE A DEEP BREATH,

TO HEAR THE WIND CALL MY NAME,

I LISTEN WITH ANTICIPATION,

WHILE THE RUSTLING OF THE WATER,

RUSHES OVER ME,

LIFTING ME INTO ITS GENTLE ARMS,

CARESSING ME SOFTLY,

TO NOT LET GO,

I TAKE CAREFUL PRIDE,

NOT TO SUMMON MOTHER NATURE,

WHILE SHE IS WORKING,

TENDERLY CALLING ME TO HER,

MY BODY RENEWS ITSELF,

WITH HER WARM SPIRIT,

RUSHING OVER ME,

LIKE A TRAIN THAT IS LATE,

THE RIPPLING OF THE WAVES,

My Soul

ARE SLOW WITH MY BODY,

TO CLEANSE EVERY PART OF ME,

I AM SLOWLY DRAWN,

TO THE BLANKET OF THE EARTH,

COVERING ME WITH ITS SPIRIT,

I GENTLY CLOSE MY EYES,

TO EMBRACE EVERY PART,

SHE HAS GIVEN ME,

TO SAVOUR EVERY PORTION,

OF OFFERING,

TO PROTECT HER,

AND TO SAVE ME!!!!!

Dawn Brown

NATURE

THE SWEET SONG OF A BLUEBIRD,

THE DIFFERENT TONES OF THE LEAVES,

SWAYING IN THE TREES,

THE CRYSTAL REFLECTION OF THE SEA,

THE CRIES OF THE NIGHT,

THE WHISPERS OF THE WIND,

THE ANIMALS HUNTING FOR THEIR YOUNG,

THE LIMBS CRACKLING WITH EVERY STEP,

THE MOONBEAMS THAT KISS THE SEA,

STANDING ON A MOUNTAIN,

TAKING IN ALL ITS BEAUTY,

THIS THE TRUTH OF NATURE!!!!!

MOTHER EARTH

SUN'S RAYS ARE BEAMING,

AS BRIGHT AS RAW DIAMONDS

SHADOWING ME,

WITH ITS ARMS OF WARMTH,

CREEPING,

EVER SO SILENTLY,

TO CAPTURE ME,

TO DRAW ME AWAY FROM THE EARTHLY MOTHER,

SISTERLY WAVES,

ARE COMING TO GREET ME,

TENDERLY,

I WELCOME THEM,

TO CLEANSE MY BODY,

MY SOUL,

MY SPIRIT,

BEING CAREFUL TO REACH DEEP WITHIN,

THE WARMTH OF THE RAYS,

THE COOLNESS OF THE WAVES,

WILL RENEW ALL OF ME,

I WILL BE ABLE TO RETURN TO THE EARTHLY MOTHER,

AS FRESH AS A NEWBORN BABY,

TO SHOW,

THE LOVE,

THE MAGIC,

THE BEAUTY,

THAT SURROUNDS US ALL!!!!!

CONCLUSION

Dawn Brown

I WILL NOT LOOSE

THE PAINS OF THE PAST,

COME INTO FOCUS,

TO SHATTER MY DREAMS,

TO DESTROY MY HOPE,

FORCING ITSELF,

TO TAKE AWAY EVERYTHING,

I HOLD ON,

WITH EVERY STRENGTH,

I HAVE LEFT,

NOT TO LET IT DESTROY,

MY EXISTENCE,

NOW THAT I HAVE FOUND,

THE BEING OF ME,

EVEN THOUGH THE WAR CONTINUES,

I AM STRONGER,

WITH NATURES CONFIDENCE,

I WILL NOT LOOSE!!!!!

THE ACCEPTANCE

THE ACCEPTANCE OF SELF IS A WAR WITH ITSELF. WE CONTINUE THE STRUGGLE, WITH RENEWAL AND CONFIDENCE. AS WE GROW, WE LEARN. WISDOM IS EARNED, AND COMMON KNOWLEDGE IS GIVEN. TO DEFY LIFE IS NOT AN OPTION. THE CHOICES WE MAKE ARE CRUCIAL TO OUR EXISTENCE. IT IS WHAT CIRCUMSTANCES WE HAVE BEEN THROUGH, THE TEST WE HAVE TAKEN THAT MAKES US WHO WE ARE. IF WE CHOOSE TO IGNORE ANYTHING IN LIFE, THEN WE ARE JUST A ZOMBIE, AND NOT HUMAN. IF WE CHOOSE TO EXPLORE ALL POSSIBILITIES, THEN WE ARE CAUTIOUS. IF WE CHOOSE TO SEEK REVENGE, THEN OUR PATH IS DESTRUCTION.

WE ALL DESERVE TO BE HAPPY IN OUR LIFE, BUT WE MUST LEARN TO FACE CHALLENGES, AND OBSTACLES BEFORE WE CAN ENJOY. THIS MAY SEEM HARSH, BUT HOW ARE WE TO KNOW WHAT IS HAPPINESS IF WE DO NOT KNOW PAIN. TO ACCOMPLISH WHAT WE WANT TO ACHIEVE OUT OF LIFE WE MUST FIRST FACE THE CHALLENGES. WE MUST TAKE THE TESTS THAT ARE GIVEN.

GOD HAS GIVEN US LIFE, BUT HE CAN ALSO TAKE IT AWAY. HE GIVES THESE CHALLENGES TO MAKE US STRONGER AND MORE CONFIDENT IN OURSELF BEFORE WE FACE THE WAR OF REALITY. HE HAS A PURPOSE, FOR EACH AND EVERY ONE, AND WHEN WE ACCEPT HIM, THEN WE ARE ABLE TO FACE WHATEVER CHALLENGES COMES OUR WAY.

LIFE IS A JOURNEY, AND LOVE MAKES THE TRIP VERY WORTHWHILE. WHILE WE ARE NOT ALONE, WE ARE ALONE. ALONE

WITHIN OURSELF. THE WAR WE MUST FACE ALONE. THE TEST WE MUST TAKE OURSELF. THE CHOICE MADE, IS WITHIN OURSELF, FOR NO ONE CAN DO IT FOR US.

AS THE WORDS ARE POURED ONTO THESE PAGES, I HOPE THAT THERE IS WISDOM, AS WELL AS STRENGTH FOR ANYONE WHO CHOOSES TO READ THESE WORDS. MY LIFE HAS BEEN AN UPSIDE DOWN BATTLE FROM DAY ONE. WEIGHING ONLY 3 POUNDS AT BIRTH, MY MOTHER ABANDONED ME ANDMY OLDER BROTHER AT THE AGE OF 2 AND 4.

I HAVE LEARNED THAT EVEN THOUGH THE WAR CONTINUES, IT IS THROUGH THESE EXPERIENCES, THAT I HAVE BECOME STRONGER, WISER, AND IN MORE CONTROL THAN EVER BEFORE. I HAVE TO INCLUDE THAT GOD IS ALWAYS BY MY SIDE AS WELL AS MY HUSBAND WHO I LOVE DEARLY, BECAUSE WITHOUT THESE TWO, I NEVER WOULD HAVE MADE IT.

GOD IS THE KEY TO SURVIVAL, HE IS THE KEY TO YOUR SOUL, HE IS THE LIGHT THAT ENTERS INTO THE DARKEST MOMENTS, HE IS THE WINDOW TO KEEP OPEN AT ALL TIMES,

HE IS THE GATE TO NOT KEEP LOCKED, HE IS THE SOUL. IF WE ARE TO SURVIVE THE END TIMES, HE IS THE ONE TO KEEP WITH YOU AT ALL TIMES. DO NOT LOSE SIGHT OF WHERE YOU CAME FROM, DO NOT LOSE WHO YOU ARE, ALWAYS REMEMBER TO KEEP THE DOOR THAT LEADS TO YOUR SOUL UNLOCKED, NO MATTER WHAT THE CIRCUMSTANCES ARE.